W9-BMO-864

WEAPONS OF SCIENCE FICTION

BY JOHN HAMILTON

Visit us at

WWW.ABDOPUBLISHING.COM

Published by ABDO Publishing Company, 4940 Viking Drive, Suite 622, Edina, Minnesota 55435.
Copyright ©2007 by Abdo Consulting Group, Inc. International copyrights reserved in all countries.
No part of this book may be reproduced in any form without written permission from the publisher.
ABDO & Daughters™ is a trademark and logo of ABDO Publishing Company.

Printed in the United States.

Editor: Paul Joseph
Graphic Design: John Hamilton
Cover Design: Neil Klinepier
Cover Illustration: *Twilight of the Empire* ©1997 Don Maitz
Interior Photos and Illustrations: p 1 light saber duel, courtesy Lucasfilm Ltd.; p 4 illustration from *The War of the Worlds,* Mary Evans Picture Library; p 5 *Catchworld* ©1978 Don Maitz; p 6 iris scan, Corbis; p 7 *Doomstar* ©1985 Don Maitz; p 8 *Night Raid* ©1981 Don Maitz; p 9 cover of *The Fall of Hyperion,* courtesy Orion Publishing Group; p 10 nanotubes, NASA; p 11 nanobot, Corbis; p 12 cover of *The Andromeda Strain,* courtesy HarperCollins; p 13 *Planet in Peril* ©1987 Janny Wurts; p 14 scene from *Star Trek,* courtesy Paramount Pictures; p 15 *Berserker Base* ©1985 Janny Wurts; p 16 scene from *Star Trek: Nemesis,* courtesy Paramount Pictures; p 17 *Star Trek II: The Wrath of Khan* poster, courtesy Paramount Pictures; p 18 *Star Wars* poster, courtesy Lucasfilm Ltd.; p 19 Samuel L. Jackson, Getty Images; p 20 M4 Carbine, U.S. Army photo by Suzanne M. Day; p 21 *Twilight of the Empire* ©1997 Don Maitz; p 22 spaceship battle, Corbis; p 23 *Having a Blast* ©1988 Don Maitz; p 24 ABL system, U.S. Air Force; p 25 SDI satellite, DOD; p 26 PhaSR rifle, DOD; p 27 Predator drone, U.S. Air Force; p 28 VMADS system, DOD; p 29 technicians setting up ADS, Sandia National Laboratories.

Library of Congress Cataloging-in-Publication Data

Hamilton, John, 1959-
  Weapons of science fiction / John Hamilton.
    p. cm. -- (The World of science fiction)
  Includes index.
  ISBN-13: 978-1-59679-997-4
  ISBN-10: 1-59679-997-8
  1. Weapons--Juvenile literature. 2. Imaginary wars and battles--Juvenile literature. 3. Science fiction--History and criticism--Juvenile literature. I. Title. II. Series: Hamilton, John, 1959- World of science fiction.

  UF500.H35 2006
  623.4--dc22
                              2006016397

CONTENTS

RAY GUNS

Ray guns in science fiction are as common as pistols in a Western. Where would a cowboy be without his trusty Colt six-shooter? Likewise, how could any self-respecting future astronaut explore a new planet without a ray gun gripped in his hand?

Technically speaking, ray guns are a kind of directed energy weapon. That simply means they send, or direct, a type of energy (such as a laser beam) in a certain direction (such as toward a slavering alien fang-beast).

Directed energy weapons go by many names: ray guns, lasers, phasers, blasters, death rays, beam guns, to name just a few. They all serve the same purpose—to allow a character to project power over distance, and to showcase futuristic technology. It's the "bang" part of whiz-bang science fiction.

The first use of directed energy weapons in science fiction, or at least the most famous, may have been H. G. Wells' *The War of the Worlds*. In the 1898 novel, Earth is invaded by Martians, who lay waste to the planet with destructive "heat rays." These tripod-mounted energy beams melt metal and turn water into steam. Any person touched by a heat ray instantly bursts into flames.

Facing page: Catchworld, by Don Maitz. *Below:* An illustration from H. G. Wells' *The War of the Worlds.*

As science fiction grew in the first part of the 20th century, ray guns became more and more common. In early sci fi movies and TV shows, astronauts with ray guns blasted their enemies with bright beams of light, or lightning-like electrical arcs.

After lasers were invented in 1960, science fiction "death rays" were often changed to laser guns, especially in movies. Laser stands for *Light Amplification by Stimulated Emission of Radiation*. A laser pumps up, or stimulates, normal light so that it emits powerful beams of photons in a single direction. Unlike a flashlight, which has a wide and scattered beam, a laser is narrow and intense.

Powerful industrial lasers can cut through steel, yet they are so precise that doctors often use them to perform delicate eye surgery. It is easy to find lasers in everyday life today, from DVD players to devices used to remove tattoos.

Particle beam weapons are similar to lasers in science fiction. Instead of light, a particle beam is an accelerated stream of atoms, called particles, that uses powerful magnets and electrostatic lenses to power and direct the energy. In real-life, a particle beam would pack a powerful punch. It would be like getting hit by billions of microscopic rocks traveling near the speed of light.

Facing page: Doomstar, by Don Maitz.
Below: Lasers are so precise they can be used to perform delicate eye surgery.

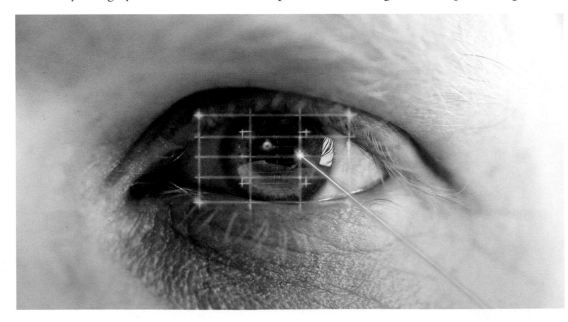

As weapons, however, lasers and particle beams have limitations that are difficult to overcome. Handheld lasers, like the small laser pointers used in lecture halls, are too weak. To make lasers and particle beam weapons strong enough to cut through, say, Imperial stormtrooper armor, you would need a huge amount of power. The battery, plus the weapon itself, would be too big for a single person to carry, at least using today's technology.

In the 1980's and 1990's, when it became apparent that lasers and particle beams might not work very well as weapons, science fiction writers and filmmakers changed their arsenals to make them sound more general, like the "blasters" of *Star Wars*. These directed energy weapons shoot bright globs of colored light or plasma. Sometimes the beams are made weak enough to stun a person instead of vaporizing them. Most of these newer ray guns shoot beams that travel much slower than the speed of light. That's why Jedi Knights can deflect blaster beams with their light sabers.

A needle gun is an interesting variation of a ray gun, and has become more popular in science fiction literature today. These weapons shoot hundreds of tiny needles, or flechettes, at very high speeds. The advantages of needle guns include very little recoil and a high rate of fire, much like ray guns. And because the needles travel so fast, they inflict a wicked amount of damage, like a shotgun. Needle guns are becoming more common in science fiction. They have been used in Dan Simmons' *Hyperion* novels, and in Harry Harrison's *Stainless Steel Rat* stories, as well as many other tales of the future.

Facing page: Night Raid, by Don Maitz.
Below: The cover of Dan Simmons' *The Fall of Hyperion.*

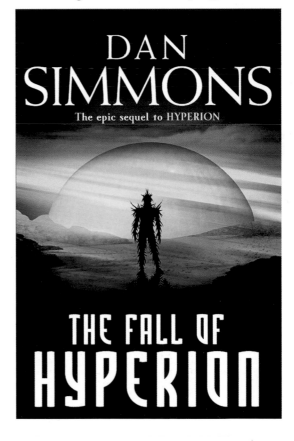

DAN SIMMONS

The epic sequel to HYPERION

THE FALL OF HYPERION

NANO WEAPONS

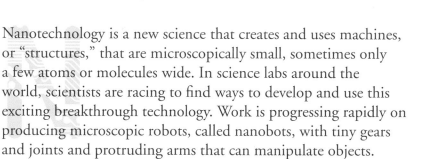

Nanotechnology is a new science that creates and uses machines, or "structures," that are microscopically small, sometimes only a few atoms or molecules wide. In science labs around the world, scientists are racing to find ways to develop and use this exciting breakthrough technology. Work is progressing rapidly on producing microscopic robots, called nanobots, with tiny gears and joints and protruding arms that can manipulate objects.

Nanobots are very, very small, less than 100 nanometers in size. One nanometer is one billionth of a meter. The width of a human hair, by comparison, is about 100 microns. (A micron is 1,000 nanometers.) That means you could line up about 1,000 nanobots and they would be about the same width as a strand of hair.

Nanotechnology may be used to make fast computer switches, or increase data storage. Tiny nanobots might someday scurry through a person's bloodstream to deliver medicine, or clear a blood clot before a fatal heart attack can strike. Unfortunately, the news isn't all-good: nanotechnology might also be used as a frightening weapon.

It's possible that future scientists will develop a kind of nanobot that's absorbed through the skin and delivers a poison to the bloodstream. Or the tiny weapons could simply start eating away at a person's cells, killing the victim from the inside out.

In Michael Crichton's 2002 novel, *Prey*, a swarm of microscopic machines escapes from a top-secret desert laboratory used by the military. Without humans to control them, the self-replicating nanobots adjust to their environment. They begin feeding on mammals, including humans. The nanobots then attack the laboratory. The out-of-control machines seem intent on killing the scientists trapped inside. It's a frightening story about the dangers of using new technology that we can't control or don't fully understand.

Facing page: A nanobot roams through a person's bloodstream. *Below:* Vertically aligned carbon nanotubes, only a few nanometers wide, grown by NASA's Ames Research Center for Nanotechnology. The tubes could someday be used to help cool computer chips.

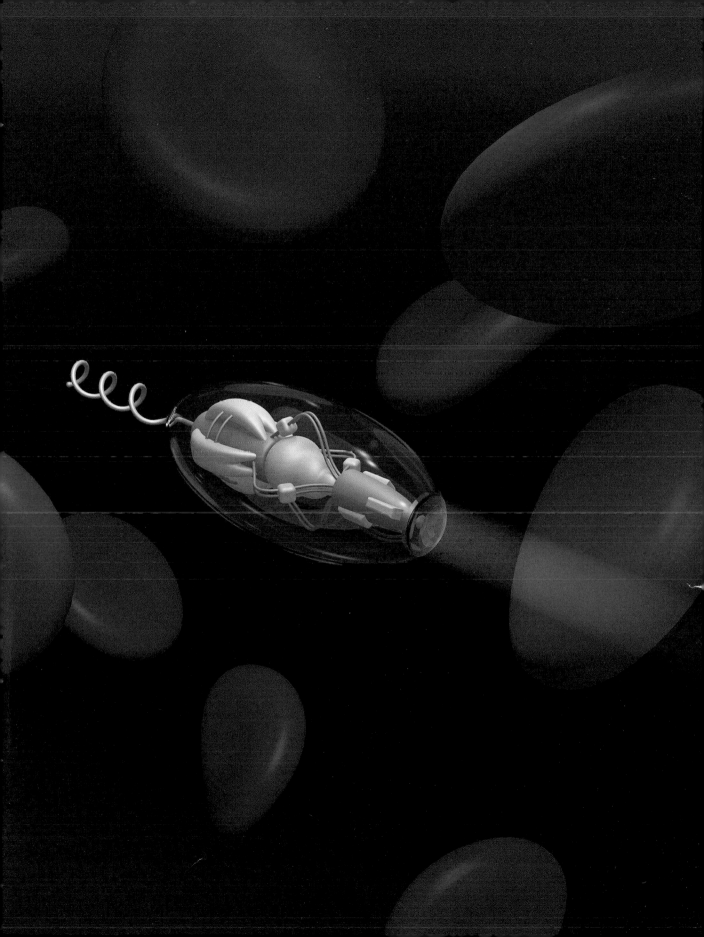

BIO WEAPONS

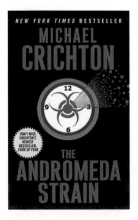

Below: The cover of Michael Crichton's bestselling techno-thriller, *The Andromeda Strain.*

Some of the most terrifying weapons of science fiction are biological, mainly because they seem so "real." In fact, there are many real-world biological agents, from anthrax, to the Ebola virus, to avian flu, that have horrified the public in recent years. It doesn't take much imagination to think that a biological weapon used in a science fiction story could someday become all too real, which makes such tales even more hair-raising.

Germ warfare has been a theme in many science fiction stories. In Terry Gilliam's 1995 film, *Twelve Monkeys*, a convict is sent back in time to stop an epidemic that wipes out five billion people. Unfortunately, he is sent back six years before the plague, and is locked up in a mental institution, having been declared insane. In both the book and movie versions of H. G. Wells' *The War of the Worlds*, the invading Martians unleash a red weed, which grows at a horrific rate. It chokes out Earth vegetation preparing the planet to be inhabited by the conquering Martians. In the 1971 movie *The Omega Man*, based on Richard Matheson's novel, *I Am Legend*, the last man on Earth roams a plague-ravaged city inhabited by mutated human-like creatures.

In some science fiction stories, the biological threat is not of this world. In the 1971 film *The Andromeda Strain*, based on the novel by Michael Crichton, a military satellite crashes to Earth with an unwanted hitchhiker from space: a deadly crystal-based virus. The virus is so lethal that people who come in contact with it die almost instantly, their blood quickly clotting and turning to dust. A team of scientists gathers at a secret underground laboratory, racing against time to deal with the alien organism before all life on Earth is wiped out.

Not all biological weapons are microscopic. In the 1979 film *Alien*, the mining freighter *Nostromo* stumbles upon a derelict spaceship containing deadly cargo, a hostile alien that kills the crew one by one in the most horrible manner imaginable.

Ripley, the sole survivor of the crew, discovers that the military on Earth knew about the aliens. They secretly sent the *Nostromo* to pick up a sample, which was to be studied back home and then used as a weapon. But the alien proves far more lethal than anyone could have imagined. It is up to Ripley to find a way to kill the alien (and hopefully escape with her life) before the creature is unleashed upon an unsuspecting Earth.

Below: Planet in Peril, by Janny Wurts.

DOOMSDAY DEVICES

The most destructive weapons of science fiction don't just kill—they destroy entire planets! These "doomsday devices" are common in science fiction, but became more frequent after the invention of nuclear weapons in the 1940s and 1950s, when people lived in constant fear of total destruction. Doomsday is a term that means "the end of the world." Science fiction doomsday devices let people explore what would happen if civilization finally destroyed itself.

In Stanley Kubrick's humorous 1964 Cold War film, *Dr. Strangelove or: How I Learned to Stop Worrying and Love the Bomb*, a mistaken American attack triggers an automatic retaliation by the Soviet Union of a "doomsday device," a bomb with such massive radioactive fallout that all life on Earth will be extinguished. A more serious treatment of this theme is explored in Nevil Shute's 1957 novel, *On the Beach*, which was made into a movie in 1959. A tragic case of mistaken identity causes the world's superpowers to wage nuclear war. World War III destroys most of civilization, except for a few remote areas in Australia. The story deals with the survivors' struggles as they await the deadly radioactive fate that slowly drifts southward toward them.

Nuclear bombs are not the only kind of planet killers in science fiction. Over the years, writers and filmmakers have devised many ways for destroying entire worlds. In 1967, science fiction author Norman Spinrad wrote a *Star Trek* episode called "The Doomsday Machine." In the story, the crew of the Starship *Enterprise* discovers a gigantic, cone-shaped machine that reduces planets to rubble and consumes them for fuel. The robotic planet killer was created by an unknown alien race. The *Enterprise's* weapons appear to be useless against the doomsday machine, which is heading towards Earth, and the crew must desperately find a way to stop it.

Below: The Starship *Constellation* confronts the planet killer in the *Star Trek* episode, "The Doomsday Machine."

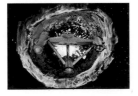

Probably the most famous planet-destroying weapon of science fiction is the Death Star from the *Star Wars* films. Built by the Empire to stop the Jedi rebellion, this moon-sized space station is capable of annihilating an entire planet with a single blast from its powerful turbolasers.

Above: Berserker Base, by Janny Wurts.

THE WEAPONS OF STAR TREK

A phaser from *Star Trek*.

The phaser is the classic weapon of the *Star Trek* television series and movies. Some say the term stands for *PHASed Energy Rectification*, but it is almost certainly a more futuristic variation of the word "laser." Phasers are particle beam weapons that shoot a type of matter called nadions. They cause the nuclear structure of a target to be disrupted. If the power is set high enough, the target is completely vaporized. Phasers can also be set at low power to merely stun a target.

The most common phasers are hand-held, about the size of a modern-day cell phone. They can be inserted into a more powerful pistol-grip, and in some cases come in a larger rifle-like configuration. The most powerful phasers are found on starships, like the *Enterprise*. They can be fired at other spaceships, or at targets on the surface of a planet. Alien races in the *Star Trek* universe have developed similar weapons to the phaser, such as the Klingon disruptor.

Starfleet vessels, in addition to ship-mounted phasers, are also armed with photon torpedoes. These powerful weapons are shot at sublight speed. They can track an enemy by using their own navigation system, much like today's guided missiles. Once they reach their target, photon torpedoes detonate by mixing matter and antimatter together, which causes a powerful explosion.

Left: A scene from *Star Trek: Nemesis* (2002), showing the *Enterprise* crew firing phaser rifles.
Facing page: A movie lobby poster for *Star Trek II: The Wrath of Khan* (1982).

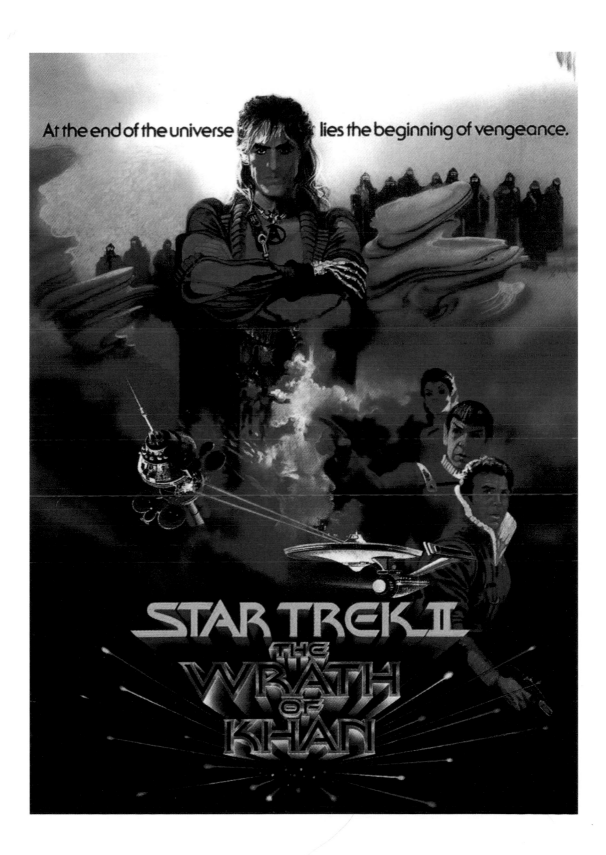

THE WEAPONS OF STAR WARS

A stormtrooper blaster.

Star Wars contains a dizzying array of futuristic weapons, from hand-held blasters to planet-killing Death Stars. Director-producer George Lucas set out to create a fictional universe that harkens back to the early science fiction days of Buck Rogers and Flash Gordon. The weapons his characters use are nods to those early stories as well; they're old-fashioned, but with a modern twist. Crossbows are replaced by Wookie bowcasters that launch energy bolts. Hand grenades become thermal detonators, mini-fusion bombs capable of enormous damage.

A *Star Wars* blaster is a hand-held particle beam weapon that fires a brightly colored bolt of energy. Like futuristic assault rifles or machine pistols, blasters can fire single shots, or be set to spray in multi-fire mode. The standard Republic clone trooper carries a DC-15 blaster rifle.

Larger blasters can also be mounted on vehicles, including spaceships. The really big spaceship weapons, however, include laser cannons, proton torpedoes, turbolasers, and ion cannons. These industrial-strength blasters are powerful enough to lay waste to entire planets. Death Stars are armed with world-destroying turbolasers.

Facing page: Samuel L. Jackson, as Jedi Knight Mace Windu, wields a light saber in this publicity photo for *Star Wars: Episode II – Attack of the Clones. Below:* A theater lobby poster for *Star Wars: Episode IV – A New Hope.*

By far the most famous *Star Wars* weapon is the light saber. A light saber is like a sword with a blade of glowing, colored light. This highly focused loop of energy can cut through almost anything, except another light saber. It takes years of intense training to use a light saber. They are usually seen only in the skilled hands of Jedi Knights or Sith Lords, such as Luke Skywalker or Darth Vader.

SCIENCE FICTION VS. REAL WEAPONS

Facing page: Twilight of the Empire, by Don Maitz.
Below: A U.S. Army M4 Carbine, preferred by U.S. Special Forces teams.

When you compare real-life weapons with the most common weapons of science fiction, you come to an uncomfortable conclusion: most modern-day weapons are deadlier and far more destructive. Take, for example, the science fiction workhorse, the ray gun/phaser/blaster: the number of times you can shoot per second, the weapon's rate of fire, is frustratingly slow. The colored rays or plasma bursts easily give away the shooter's location. And the weapons are very hard to aim. If Imperial stormtroopers are such good shots, how come they miss their targets so often? Even an army of drones in *Star Wars: Episode II – Attack of the Clones,* it seemed, couldn't hit the broad side of a barn.

By contrast, compare a modern military rifle, such as the M4 Carbine, preferred by U.S. Special Forces teams. It has an incredible rate of fire (more than 12 shots *per second*), capable of ripping an enemy to shreds. It can also be fitted with attachments that let soldiers see in the dark, use red-dot laser pointers, or

fire high-explosive grenades. Even a Jedi Knight would be helpless against a trained squad of soldiers armed with such fearsome weapons.

But it's not really fair to criticize science-fiction weapons too much, especially those seen in movies. The weapons in sci fi films are made for visual impact—they don't reflect reality. Slow, colorful bursts of energy coming from a *Star Wars*-type blaster make for exciting cinema, even if it's unrealistic.

Above: A Frank R. Paul illustration of a spaceship battle on the Moon.

Truly advanced weapons are more often found in science fiction *books*, especially realistic *hard science fiction*. Even in softer science fiction, such as the *Hyperion* series of books by Dan Simmons, weapons are often described that are frighteningly lethal. In *Hyperion*, the heroes confront the Shrike, a huge four-armed, metal-clad, razor-and-spike covered god-machine whose purpose is to create pain and suffering.

Where science fiction weapons really have an advantage is in the cold vacuum of space. Because ray guns fire beams of energy, they don't have the recoil problem that projectile weapons would have. Physicist Isaac Newton's Third Law of Motion states that for every action, there is an equal but opposite reaction. That's why a gun recoils backward when fired.

If you were floating in the weightless environment of space and fired a gun, you would be pushed backward by the recoil. Since there's no gravity or atmosphere to stop you, you would keep going forever until you applied yet another force in the opposite direction, perhaps by firing some kind of retro-rocket. Recoil is a serious problem, and would make shooting a gun in space extremely difficult.

Another problem would be the weight of the ammunition you would have to carry in space. Ray guns would not have this weight problem, except perhaps for extra battery packs. For a starship, not having to carry tons of ammunition would be a huge advantage.

A final advantage of a science fiction "death ray" is that it would travel at the speed of light. For all practical purposes, it would strike its target instantaneously.

Above: Having a Blast, by Don Maitz.

FUTURE WEAPONS

Like the high-powered spaceship blasters of science fiction, a real-life laser or particle-beam weapon used in space could be highly effective. The United States is now working on such weapons. They are part of the Strategic Defense Initiative (SDI), which is commonly nicknamed Star Wars, after the movie. One part of SDI would use a system of powerful lasers, either mounted on satellites or high-flying airplanes, to knock down enemy missiles.

Scientists are also hard at work on futuristic weapons for use here on Earth. The military is developing a high-energy laser cannon that uses mirrors to focus its deadly beam. The Mobile Tactical High Energy Laser (MTHEL) uses a special liquid to cool the weapon to prevent overheating. Once its tracking system detects a missile, it fires a deuterium-fluoride laser beam at the target. The laser beam is only a few inches in diameter, but it heats the missile's shell so much that the target explodes in mid-air.

At the moment, MTHEL is so big that it can only be used on the ground, or carried on very large planes. But as development continues, it will likely be made small enough to be equipped on small planes, tanks, and ships. The U.S. Army is testing a similar Humvee-mounted weapon, called Zeus.

Left: An illustration of the U.S. Air Force Airborne Laser (ABL) system. Mounted on the nose of specially modified 747 aircraft, the lasers will be able to destroy enemy missiles up to several hundred kilometers away.
Facing page: An artist's conception of a space-based laser defense satellite.

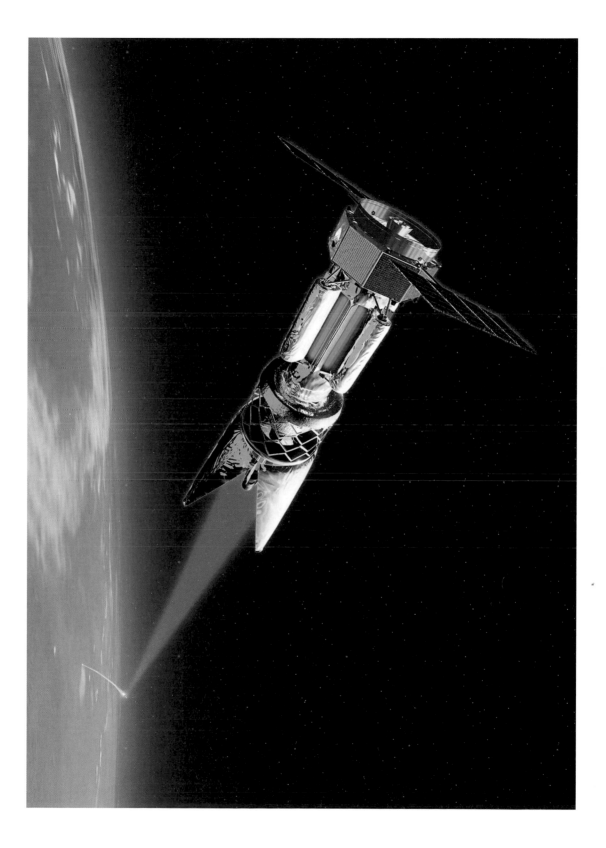

Future foot-soldiers might use ray guns or particle beam weapons, but there are obstacles that must be overcome. Most importantly, the weapons require huge amounts of energy, which current battery technology can't supply.

One interesting, yet horrifying, energy beam weapon once considered would use rapid pulses of high-powered lasers to sweep over a battlefield. Since the human eye is very sensitive to laser light, the weapon would blind enemy troops. Such an inhumane weapon, however, is banned under international treaties. Not only that, it would be very difficult to prevent some of *our own* troops from being accidentally blinded. One solution is a rifle-like weapon developed by the U.S. Air Force. Called a PhaSR rifle (Personnel Halting and Stimulation Response), it uses a lower-powered laser to merely "dazzle" enemy troops or rioters, only temporarily blinding them. Its long-term effects, however, are still being studied.

Below: A researcher fires a PhaSR rifle, which uses a laser to temporarily blind enemy troops.

Left: A U.S. Air Force Predator unmanned drone, with a powerful missile carried under its wing.

Many future weapons wouldn't require human soldiers at all. The U.S. military is hard at work developing robots that can defuse bombs, sniff out enemy soldiers, and even wield machine guns. These mechanical soldiers could be joystick-controlled by a remote operator miles away. Some weapons already in use today, such as high-flying Predator drones, can be controlled through satellite links by ground operators on another continent. Future drones may be as small as insects, with tiny cameras for "eyes." These could be sent into the air by soldiers in battle, who could scout enemy positions by watching the video-feed on iPod-like portable viewing screens.

Non-lethal weapons, such as freeze guns or stun rays, are often seen in science fiction. There are many examples of such weapons already in use by today's police forces. Stun guns disable people by using electric shock to disrupt muscle functions. Taser is a well-known brand of stun gun.

An even lower-tech form of non-lethal weapon is simple pepper spray. It is made of a liquid containing capsaicin, which is found in the fruit of certain kinds of plants, such as chili peppers. Sprayed into the face, it causes eyes to water and throat and nasal airways to tighten up. It is very effective in controlling riots, or other situations where police do not wish to kill people but need a way to manage violent crowds.

Other non-lethal weapons in development include stink bombs, quick-hardening foam that can be sprayed on rioters, microwave beams, and sonic weapons that cause disorientation or break eardrums. The U.S. Army today uses the Long-Range Acoustic Device (LRAD) to beam both messages and painful, screeching noise into hostile crowds.

The Army's experimental Pulsed Energy Projectile (PEP) shoots intense pulses of laser energy into crowds. These invisible plasma explosions create shockwaves that cause temporary paralysis. Nerve cells are triggered in people targeted by PEP, which makes them feel intense burning sensations, or pressure, or even cold. A similar weapon, the Active Denial System (ADS), sometimes known as Project Sheriff, beams powerful electromagnetic energy into a hostile crowd. The beam causes disabling pain by triggering heat receptors in the skin. People stop what they're doing and flinch, much like when you accidentally touch a stove or burning match. Wade Smith is a director for Raytheon, the company that manufactures the Sheriff for the Army. In an interview with the *Arizona Daily Star* newspaper, Smith said, "This is an effect that literally gets under your skin. I can assure you, once you come in contact with the beam, you will be inclined to stop whatever you are doing."

The PEP and ADS weapons are remarkably similar to author Isaac Asimov's neuronic whip, which he describes in *The Stars, Like Dust,* published in 1951: "…the path of the beam intersected Biron's foot. It was as though he had stepped into a bath of boiling lead. Or as if a granite block had toppled upon it. Or as if it had been crunched off by a shark. Actually, nothing had happened to it physically. It was only that the nerve endings that governed the sensation of pain had been universally and maximally stimulated."

Below: An ADS mounted on a military vehicle.

There are many other examples of real-life weapons similar to those found in novels and movies. Some work well, others are only experimental—for now. It's obvious, though, that as the technology of weapons marches on, science fact is rapidly catching up with science fiction.

Above: Two Sandia National Laboratories technicians set up an Active Denial System (ADS), which can beam powerful electromagnetic beams at people.

GLOSSARY

ANTIMATTER

A kind of matter that has the exact opposite electrical charge as matter found in our universe. If a piece of matter and antimatter collided, pure energy would be released. Some scientists speculate that it may be possible to open a kind of "window" into alternate universes where antimatter exists. If antimatter could somehow be contained and harnessed, it could be used as a clean and efficient fuel for future spaceships.

CLONE

An organism that is "grown" from donor cells, making an exact copy of the original.

COLD WAR

The mainly diplomatic conflict waged between the United States and the former Soviet Union after World War II. The Cold War resulted in a large buildup of weapons and troops. It ended when the Soviet Union broke up in the late 1980s and early 1990s.

DIRECTED ENERGY WEAPON

A kind of weapon that sends, or directs, energy in a certain direction. Common science fiction names for directed energy weapons include ray guns, lasers, phasers, death rays, and blasters.

DOOMSDAY

A term that means "the end of the world." Doomsday devices became more common in science fiction stories after the invention of nuclear weapons in the late 1940s and early 1950s.

HARD SCIENCE FICTION

Science fiction that emphasizes facts and reality. Hard science fiction is filled with scientific detail. It tries to present a realistic speculation of how science will affect future societies.

LASER

A beam of directed energy. Laser light contains photons that are lined up in a single direction, rather than scattered like normal light. Laser light can be so powerful that it can burn through metal, yet precise enough so that doctors can perform delicate eye surgery. The word laser stands for "Light Amplification by Stimulated Emission of Radiation."

LIGHT SPEED

Light travels at a speed of approximately 186,282 miles per second (299,792 km/sec).

NANOMETER

One billionth of a meter. One micron equals 1,000 nanometers. A human hair is about 100 microns wide.

NASA

The National Aeronautics and Space Administration. NASA is the United States' main space agency, responsible for programs such as the Space Shuttle and unmanned space probes.

RECOIL

When a gun is fired, it moves back abruptly. This recoil effect can be quite violent. For example, unless a person is properly braced, a powerful shotgun can knock a shooter down. Directed energy weapons, like lasers, have no recoil, and would be better suited for space battles. A gun fired in space would send an astronaut hurtling backward forever until an equal amount of force was applied in the opposite direction.

SOFT SCIENCE FICTION

Science fiction that emphasizes plot and characters more than scientific detail and realism. Space operas such as *Star Wars* are often considered soft science fiction. For example, space battles in *Star Wars* feature noisy and fiery explosions, impossible in the airless vacuum of space.

INDEX